Prioritize Prayer:

The Importance of Making Prayer One's Life Foundation

by

Alan S. Rodriguez

Introduction

The introduction of "Prioritizing Prayer: The Art of Making Prayer the Foundation of Your Life" sets the tone for the book and provides an overview of its purpose and content. The introduction is intended to capture the reader's interest, engage them with the topic of prayer, and explain why the book is relevant and important to their spiritual life. It may also introduce the author and their personal experience with prayer.

In the introduction, the author may discuss the significance of prayer as a foundational aspect of spiritual life, emphasizing the benefits of prayer, such as peace, wisdom, and connection to a higher power. They may also explain the purpose of the book, which is to help readers prioritize prayer in their daily lives and to provide practical guidance for developing and deepening a prayer practice. The introduction may also highlight some of the key themes and sections of the book to give the reader an idea of what to expect from the content. Ultimately, the introduction should leave the reader feeling inspired and motivated to engage with the book and to make prayer a priority in their own lives.

The Importance of Prayer

Prayer is an essential component of spiritual life for many people around the world. It is a way to connect with a higher power, express gratitude, seek guidance, and find inner peace. Prayer can be defined as a conversation with God, a moment of introspection, or a form of meditation. Regardless of how it is defined, prayer has numerous benefits that make it an important practice for spiritual growth and well-being.

One of the main benefits of prayer is that it helps us to build a relationship with a higher power. By communicating with God or a divine force, we can feel more connected to something greater than ourselves, which can provide a sense of purpose and meaning in life.

Prayer can also help us to express gratitude for the blessings in our lives and to ask for help in times of need.

In addition to the spiritual benefits of prayer, there are numerous emotional, physical, and social benefits as well. Studies have shown that prayer can reduce stress and anxiety, improve mood, and enhance overall well-being. Prayer can also help us to develop empathy, compassion, and forgiveness, which can improve our relationships with others.

Finally, prayer can be a powerful tool for personal growth and transformation. Through prayer, we can examine our beliefs, values, and actions, and seek to align them with our highest ideals. Prayer can help us to develop a greater sense of self-awareness, wisdom, and purpose, and to overcome challenges and obstacles in life.

Overall, prayer is a valuable practice that can help us to connect with a higher power, improve our well-being, and grow as individuals. By prioritizing prayer in our lives, we can cultivate a deeper sense of meaning, purpose, and fulfillment.

The Purpose of the Book

The purpose of the book "Prioritizing Prayer: The Art of Making Prayer the Foundation of Your Life" is to help readers develop and deepen their prayer practice, and to make prayer a priority in their daily lives. The book is designed to be a practical guide that offers guidance and inspiration for readers of all faiths and backgrounds who seek to cultivate a more meaningful and transformative prayer life.

The book provides an overview of the benefits of prayer, the different types of prayer, and the obstacles that can hinder our prayer practice. It also offers practical advice on developing a habit of prayer, cultivating the right attitude and heart for prayer, and choosing the most effective prayer methods. The book explores the power of prayer, including how it can transform our lives, improve our relationships with others, and help us to grow spiritually and emotionally.

In addition to providing guidance for individual prayer, the book also explores the importance of community prayer, and offers suggestions for joining or creating a prayer group, and being a prayer partner.

Ultimately, the goal of the book is to inspire readers to prioritize prayer in their lives, and to provide them with the tools and guidance they need to make prayer a foundational aspect of their spiritual life. Whether readers are new to prayer or have been praying for years, the book is intended to be a helpful resource that will support them in deepening their connection with a higher power and finding greater peace, purpose, and joy in life.

PART I: UNDERSTANDING PRAYER

"Prayer is not just a monologue with a higher power, but a dialogue that requires a listening heart, a humble spirit, and a willingness to understand."

Chapter 1: What is Prayer?

"Prayer is not about changing the world around us, but about changing the world within us."

This chapter provides an overview of prayer, its definition, and its different forms. It explains the meaning and purpose of prayer and explores how it can be used to connect with a higher power, express gratitude, seek guidance, and find inner peace.

The chapter begins by defining prayer and its various forms, including spoken prayer, silent prayer, meditation, and contemplation. It explores the different religious and cultural traditions that use prayer as a form of spiritual practice and highlights the commonalities among these practices.

The chapter also discusses the various motivations for prayer, including seeking blessings, expressing gratitude, asking for guidance, seeking forgiveness, and finding inner peace. It emphasizes that prayer is a personal and subjective experience that can be different for each individual.

Finally, the chapter explores the benefits of prayer, both spiritual and psychological. It highlights how prayer can help individuals to feel more connected to a higher power, to experience inner peace and emotional healing, and to develop empathy, compassion, and forgiveness.

By the end of the chapter, readers will have a better understanding of what prayer is, its different forms and motivations, and the many benefits it can offer. The chapter sets the foundation for the rest of the book, which will delve deeper into the practice of prayer and offer practical guidance for developing and deepening a prayer practice.

Defining Prayer

Prayer can be defined in many ways depending on one's spiritual or religious beliefs, cultural background, and personal experiences. Generally, prayer is a form of communication with a higher power or divine force. It is a way to express gratitude, seek guidance, make requests, or offer praise or worship.

At its core, prayer is a conversation between an individual and a higher power, whether that be God, the Universe, or another form of divinity. Through prayer, individuals can share their thoughts, feelings, and concerns with this higher power, and receive guidance or comfort in return.

Prayer can take many forms, including spoken or written words, songs, chants, or silence. It can be done individually or in groups, and can be practiced in many different settings, such as a place of worship, in nature, or in the privacy of one's own home.

For many individuals, prayer is a way to connect with a higher power and find meaning, purpose, and peace in life. It can provide a sense of comfort and support in times of difficulty, and can help to cultivate a deeper sense of gratitude and compassion for others.

Overall, prayer is a deeply personal and subjective experience that can take many different forms and serve many different purposes. Regardless of one's beliefs or practices, prayer can be a powerful tool for personal growth, emotional healing, and spiritual transformation.

The Different Types of Prayer

There are many different types of prayer that individuals can use as part of their spiritual or religious practice. Here are a few examples:

1. **Intercessory prayer:** This is a type of prayer that involves asking for divine intervention on behalf of someone else. It can be used to pray for a loved one's health, safety, or well-being.

2. **Contemplative prayer:** This type of prayer involves quieting the mind and focusing on the presence of a higher power. It can involve repeating a word or phrase, or simply sitting in silence and listening for guidance.

3. **Adoration prayer:** This type of prayer involves praising and worshiping a higher power for its goodness and greatness. It can involve singing, reciting prayers, or simply expressing gratitude and awe.

4. **Petitionary prayer:** This type of prayer involves asking a higher power for something specific, such as guidance, healing, or strength.

5. **Thankful prayer:** This type of prayer involves expressing gratitude for the blessings in one's life. It can be done in response to a specific event or situation, or as a regular practice of giving thanks.

6. **Confessional prayer:** This type of prayer involves acknowledging one's shortcomings or mistakes, and

asking for forgiveness. It can be a way to release guilt or shame and seek a path toward redemption.

7. **Liturgical prayer:** This type of prayer is part of a structured religious service or ceremony, and often involves reciting specific prayers or scripture.

8. **Meditative prayer:** This type of prayer involves using a specific meditation technique, such as focusing on the breath, to quiet the mind and connect with a higher power.

These are just a few examples of the many different types of prayer that individuals can use as part of their spiritual or religious practice. Ultimately, the type of prayer that is most effective will depend on one's personal beliefs, preferences, and intentions.

Why Prayer is Important

Prayer is important for many reasons, both spiritual and psychological. Here are a few reasons why prayer is important:

1. **Connection with a higher power:** For many individuals, prayer is a way to connect with a higher power or divine force. It can provide a sense of comfort, guidance, and support in times of difficulty, and can help individuals to feel a sense of connection and purpose in life.

2. **Gratitude and perspective:** Prayer can help individuals to cultivate a sense of gratitude for the blessings in their lives. It can also provide a perspective on the bigger picture, helping individuals to focus on what is truly important and meaningful in life.

3. **Emotional healing:** Prayer can be a powerful tool for emotional healing, allowing individuals to release negative emotions such as anger, fear, and sadness. It

can also provide a sense of inner peace and calm, reducing stress and anxiety.

4. **Community and support:** Prayer can be a way to connect with others who share similar beliefs and values. It can provide a sense of community and support, helping individuals to feel a sense of belonging and connection.

5. **Forgiveness and self-reflection:** Prayer can provide an opportunity for individuals to reflect on their actions and behaviors, and to seek forgiveness for any mistakes or wrongdoing. This can be an important step in personal growth and development.

Overall, prayer can be a powerful tool for spiritual and emotional growth and can offer many benefits to individuals who practice it regularly. By prioritizing prayer as a daily practice, individuals can deepen their connection with a higher power, cultivate a sense of gratitude and perspective, and find support and healing in times of difficulty.

Chapter 2
The Benefits of Prayer

"Prayer can calm the mind, uplift the spirit, and provide a sense of hope and peace in the midst of life's challenges. It is a powerful tool that connects us to something greater than ourselves and reminds us that we are never truly alone."

In this chapter, we will explore some of the many benefits of prayer, including its positive effects on mental, emotional, and physical health. Here are some of the key benefits of prayer:

1. **Reducing stress and anxiety:** Prayer has been shown to have a calming effect on the mind and body, reducing feelings of stress and anxiety. This can be particularly helpful for individuals who are dealing with chronic stress or anxiety disorders.

2. **Improving emotional well-being:** Regular prayer can help to improve overall emotional well-being, by providing a sense of comfort, support, and guidance. It can also help to reduce symptoms of depression, and increase feelings of hope and optimism.

3. **Enhancing spiritual connection:** Prayer can help individuals to feel more connected to a higher power or divine force, deepening their sense of spirituality and purpose in life.

4. **Boosting self-esteem:** Prayer can help individuals to feel more confident in themselves and their abilities, increasing feelings of self-worth and self-esteem.

5. **Improving physical health:** Research has shown that prayer can have positive effects on physical

health, including reducing blood pressure, improving immune function, and decreasing the risk of chronic diseases such as heart disease and cancer.

6. **Fostering positive relationships:** Prayer can be a way to connect with others who share similar beliefs and values, building positive relationships and a sense of community.

7. **Cultivating gratitude:** Regular prayer can help individuals to cultivate a sense of gratitude for the blessings in their lives, improving overall feelings of happiness and life satisfaction.

Overall, the benefits of prayer are numerous and can have a significant impact on an individual's mental, emotional, and physical well-being. By prioritizing prayer as a daily practice, individuals can improve their overall quality of life and deepen their connection to themselves, others, and a higher power.

Spiritual Benefits

In addition to the physical and emotional benefits, prayer can also have profound spiritual benefits. Here are some of the key spiritual benefits of prayer:

1. **Deepening spiritual connection:** One of the primary spiritual benefits of prayer is the deepening of an individual's spiritual connection to a higher power or divine force. Regular prayer can help individuals to feel more connected to their sense of purpose and to the world around them.

2. **Developing greater awareness and mindfulness:** Prayer can help individuals to develop greater awareness and mindfulness in their daily lives. By taking time to reflect on their thoughts and feelings, individuals can become more present in the moment and more attuned to their own needs and the needs of others.

3. **Cultivating a sense of humility:** Prayer can help individuals to cultivate a sense of humility and a recognition of their own limitations. This can be an important step in developing empathy and compassion for others, and in recognizing the interconnectedness of all beings.

4. **Promoting inner peace and calm:** Regular prayer can help individuals to cultivate a sense of inner peace and calm, even in the midst of difficult circumstances. This can be an important tool for managing stress and anxiety and for maintaining a sense of equanimity in the face of life's challenges.

5. **Encouraging personal growth and transformation:** Prayer can be a powerful tool for personal growth and transformation, by encouraging individuals to reflect on their actions and behaviors, seek forgiveness for past mistakes, and set intentions for the future.

6. **Strengthening faith and trust:** Regular prayer can help to strengthen an individual's faith and trust in a higher power or divine force. This can provide a sense of comfort and support during times of difficulty, and can help individuals to maintain a sense of hope and optimism in the face of adversity.\

Overall, the spiritual benefits of prayer can be profound and can help individuals to cultivate a deeper sense of connection, awareness, and purpose in their lives. By prioritizing prayer as a daily practice, individuals can experience a greater sense of inner peace, personal growth, and spiritual fulfillment.

Emotional Benefits

1. **Providing comfort and solace:** Prayer can be a source of comfort and solace in times of emotional distress. It can provide a safe space to express one's

feelings and to seek comfort from a higher power or divine force.

2. **Reducing anxiety and stress:** Regular prayer can help to reduce feelings of anxiety and stress, which can be particularly helpful for individuals dealing with chronic stress or anxiety disorders.

3. **Improving mood and emotional wellbeing:** Prayer can help to improve overall mood and emotional well-being by providing a sense of support, guidance, and hope. It can also help to reduce symptoms of depression and increase feelings of joy and contentment.

4. **Enhancing self-awareness:** Through prayer, individuals can become more aware of their own emotions, thoughts, and behaviors. This can help to cultivate greater self-awareness and self-acceptance, leading to improved emotional wellbeing.

5. **Strengthening relationships:** Prayer can be a way to connect with others who share similar beliefs and

values, building positive relationships and a sense of community. This can help to reduce feelings of isolation and loneliness, which can contribute to poor emotional health.

6. **Cultivating forgiveness and compassion:** Prayer can be a tool for cultivating forgiveness and compassion for oneself and others. This can be an important step in improving emotional well-being, by letting go of negative emotions and promoting positive ones.

Overall, the emotional benefits of prayer can be significant and can help individuals to improve their overall emotional well-being, reduce stress and anxiety, and cultivate positive relationships with themselves and others.

Physical Benefits

Prayer can also have several physical benefits, including:

1. **Reducing stress and anxiety:** Prayer can help to reduce feelings of stress and anxiety, which can have a positive impact on physical health. Chronic stress and anxiety have been linked to a range of health problems, including high blood pressure, heart disease, and obesity.

2. **Boosting the immune system:** Prayer has been shown to boost the immune system, which can help individuals to fight off infections and illnesses. It has been linked to an increase in white blood cells, which are essential for fighting off viruses and bacteria.

3. **Improving sleep:** Regular prayer can help individuals to improve the quality of their sleep. It can promote feelings of relaxation and calm, which can make it easier to fall asleep and stay asleep throughout the night.

4. **Lowering blood pressure:** Prayer has been shown to lower blood pressure, which can reduce the risk of heart disease and stroke. High blood pressure is a

major risk factor for cardiovascular disease, which is one of the leading causes of death worldwide.

5. **Relieving pain:** Prayer has been shown to have pain-relieving effects, which can be particularly helpful for individuals dealing with chronic pain. It can help to reduce feelings of discomfort and improve the overall quality of life.

6. **Improving overall health and longevity:** Regular prayer has been linked to improved overall health and longevity. It can help individuals to maintain a healthy weight, reduce their risk of chronic diseases, and improve their overall quality of life.

Overall, the physical benefits of prayer can be significant and can help individuals to improve their overall health and well-being. By incorporating prayer into their daily routine, individuals can experience reduced stress and anxiety, better sleep, improved immune function, and a lower risk of chronic diseases.

Social Benefits

Prayer can also have several social benefits, including:

1. **Building a sense of community:** Prayer can be a way to connect with others who share similar beliefs and values, building a sense of community and belonging. It can provide opportunities for individuals to meet and interact with others in a safe and supportive environment.

2. **Strengthening relationships:** Prayer can be a way to strengthen relationships with family and friends. It can provide opportunities for individuals to express gratitude, seek forgiveness, and offer support to those around them.

3. **Fostering empathy and compassion:** Through prayer, individuals can develop empathy and compassion for others. It can help to promote a sense

of understanding and acceptance, and to encourage individuals to help others in need.

4. **Providing a sense of purpose:** Prayer can provide individuals with a sense of purpose and direction in life. It can help individuals to identify their values and priorities, and to work towards fulfilling their goals and aspirations.

5. **Promoting ethical behavior:** Prayer can be a way to promote ethical behavior and moral values. It can encourage individuals to act with integrity and honesty, and to make decisions based on their beliefs and values.

6. **Enhancing social support:** Prayer can provide individuals with a source of social support and encouragement. It can be a way to seek guidance and support from a higher power or divine force, and to feel connected to something larger than oneself.

Overall, the social benefits of prayer can be significant and can help individuals to build positive relationships, develop empathy and compassion for others, and promote ethical behavior and moral values. By incorporating prayer into their daily routine, individuals can experience a greater sense of community, purpose, and social support.

Chapter 3
The Obstacles to Prayer

"The noise of the world, the distractions of the mind, and the busyness of life can all be obstacles to prayer. But when we make the effort to overcome these obstacles, we

can find a deeper connection to our inner selves and to the divine."

In this chapter, we will explore some of the obstacles that can make it difficult to establish and maintain a consistent prayer practice. These obstacles can include:

1. **Lack of time:** One of the most common obstacles to prayer is a lack of time. Many individuals lead busy lives and may struggle to find the time to set aside for prayer.

2. **Distractions:** In today's world, there are countless distractions that can make it difficult to focus on prayer. These can include electronic devices, social media, and other forms of entertainment.

3. **Doubt and skepticism:** Some individuals may struggle with doubt and skepticism when it comes to prayer. They may question whether prayer is effective, or whether a higher power exists.

4. **Negative experiences:** Individuals who have had negative experiences with religion or prayer in the past may be hesitant to engage in prayer in the present.

5. **Lack of motivation:** Some individuals may struggle with a lack of motivation to pray. They may not see the value in prayer, or may struggle to establish a consistent practice.

6. **Guilt and shame:** Individuals who feel guilty or ashamed about their past actions or behaviors may struggle to connect with a higher power or may feel unworthy of prayer.

By understanding these obstacles and identifying which ones are relevant to our individual situations, we can begin to develop strategies for overcoming them and establishing a more consistent prayer practice. With dedication and persistence, we can overcome these obstacles and experience the many benefits that prayer has to offer.

Common Challenges in Prayer

In addition to the obstacles to prayer discussed in the previous chapter, there are also several common challenges that individuals may face when engaging in prayer. These challenges can include:

1. **Difficulty focusing:** Many individuals may struggle to maintain their focus during prayer, particularly if they are new to the practice. This can be especially challenging for those who are easily distracted or who have busy minds.

2. **Lack of variety:** Praying, in the same way, every day can become monotonous and unfulfilling. A lack of variety can also make prayer feel like a chore.

3. **Feeling disconnected:** Individuals may feel disconnected from their higher power or the divine

during prayer. This can be due to feelings of doubt, skepticism, or unresolved issues.

4. **Lack of progress:** When individuals feel like they are not making progress in their prayer practice, they may become discouraged and lose motivation.

5. **Guilt and shame:** Some individuals may struggle with feelings of guilt and shame during prayer, particularly if they feel like they are not living up to their own or others' expectations.

6. **Comparison:** Comparing one's own prayer practice to that of others can be a challenge. It can lead to feelings of inadequacy or self-judgment.

7. **Burnout:** Engaging in prayer for an extended period of time without breaks or rest can lead to burnout. This can result in individuals feeling emotionally and physically exhausted.

By recognizing these common challenges and developing strategies for addressing them, individuals can continue to deepen their prayer practice and experience its many benefits. This can include incorporating variety into their practice, seeking guidance or support from others, and taking breaks when needed. With dedication and perseverance, individuals can overcome these challenges and find meaning and connection through prayer.

How to Overcome Obstacles to Prayer

Overcoming obstacles to prayer can be challenging, but with patience and persistence, it is possible. Here are some strategies that can be used to overcome common obstacles to prayer:

1. **Lack of time:** If lack of time is an obstacle to prayer, try setting aside a specific time each day for prayer. This can be early in the morning, during lunch break, or before bed. Scheduling a regular time for prayer can help make it a habit and easier to prioritize.

2. **Distractions:** To overcome distractions during prayer, consider finding a quiet, secluded place where you can pray without interruptions. Turning off electronic devices, like phones or televisions, can also help limit distractions.

3. **Doubt and skepticism:** Overcoming doubt and skepticism can be challenging, but it can be helpful to approach prayer with an open mind and heart. Consider exploring different prayer traditions, or seeking guidance from a trusted spiritual mentor or teacher.

4. **Negative experiences:** If negative experiences with prayer or religion are an obstacle, consider exploring new approaches to prayer or seeking out a new spiritual community that aligns with your values and beliefs.

5. **Lack of motivation:** To overcome a lack of motivation, it can be helpful to remind yourself of the benefits of prayer, like greater peace of mind,

increased clarity and focus, and deeper connection to a higher power. It can also be helpful to set goals and track your progress in your prayer practice.

6. **Guilt and shame:** To overcome feelings of guilt and shame, it can be helpful to practice self-compassion and forgiveness. Remember that everyone makes mistakes, and that prayer can be a powerful tool for healing and growth.

By incorporating these strategies into your prayer practice, you can overcome obstacles and develop a deeper, more fulfilling relationship with prayer. Remember that prayer is a personal journey, and there is no "right" or "wrong" way to pray. With dedication and persistence, you can develop a prayer practice that feels meaningful and authentic to you.

PART II: DEVELOPING A PRAYER LIFE

"Developing a prayer life is not about being perfect, it's about showing up authentically and consistently, with an open heart and a willingness to grow."

Chapter 4
The Habit of Prayer

"Prayer is not a one-time event, but a daily habit that can transform our lives, renew our minds, and inspire our souls."

In this chapter, we will explore the importance of developing a regular prayer habit. We will discuss how to make prayer a part of your daily routine, the benefits of a consistent prayer practice, and strategies for overcoming obstacles to building a prayer habit. We will also explore different prayer techniques and rituals that can help deepen your connection to the divine and enhance the spiritual benefits of prayer.

Developing a Habit of Prayer

Developing a habit of prayer can be a transformative experience that can lead to greater peace of mind, increased spiritual connection, and a deeper sense of purpose in life. Here are some strategies for building a consistent prayer practice:

1. **Set aside a specific time for prayer each day:** Whether it's in the morning, at lunchtime, or before bed, setting aside a specific time each day for prayer can help make it a habit.

2. **Create a sacred space for prayer:** Having a dedicated space for prayer, like a quiet corner of your home or a special room, can help create a sense of ritual and intention around your prayer practice.

3. **Start small:** If you're new to prayer or building a prayer habit, start with a few minutes each day and gradually build up to longer periods of time.

4. **Find a prayer partner or community:** Having a partner or community to pray with can provide accountability, support, and inspiration.

5. **Try different prayer techniques and rituals:** Experimenting with different prayer techniques, like meditation, visualization, or reciting sacred texts, can help keep your prayer practice fresh and engaging.

Remember that building a habit of prayer takes time and patience, and that it's okay to experience setbacks or challenges along the way. The most important thing is to approach prayer with an open heart and a willingness to grow, and to make prayer a regular part of your daily routine.

Creating a Prayer Schedule

Creating a prayer schedule can be a helpful tool for building a consistent prayer habit. Here are some steps for creating a prayer schedule:

1. **Decide on the frequency and duration of your prayer sessions:** Determine how often you want to pray each day or week, and how long you want each prayer session to last.

2. **Choose a specific time for each prayer session:** Decide on a specific time for each prayer session, and try to stick to this time as much as possible.

3. **Identify the type of prayer you want to engage in:** Decide on the type of prayer you want to engage in during each session, such as meditation, reciting prayers or affirmations, or reading sacred texts.

4. **Create a ritual around your prayer practice:** Consider incorporating a specific ritual or activity to help create a sense of intention and focus around your prayer practice, such as lighting candles or burning incense.

5. **Be flexible:** Be willing to adjust your prayer schedule as needed, based on changes in your schedule or other circumstances.

Remember that creating a prayer schedule is not about being rigid or inflexible, but about creating a structure that can help support your prayer practice and make it a consistent part of your daily routine. Be open to experimentation and change, and always approach your prayer practice with an open heart and a spirit of curiosity and learning.

Chapter 5
The Heart of Prayer

"The heart of prayer is not in the words we say, but in the intention behind them - the longing, the gratitude, the surrender, and the love that we bring to each moment of connection with the divine."

In this chapter, we will explore the deeper dimensions of prayer and how it can serve as a powerful tool for cultivating a heart-centered approach to life. We will discuss the importance of intention, gratitude, surrender, and love in prayer, and how these qualities can transform our relationship with ourselves, others, and the divine. We will also explore the role of prayer in cultivating inner peace, resilience, and wisdom, and how it can help us navigate the challenges and uncertainties of life with greater clarity and purpose.

The Attitude of Prayer

One of the most important aspects of prayer is the attitude with which we approach it. A positive and open attitude can help us cultivate a deeper sense of connection with the divine, while a negative or closed attitude can hinder our ability to access the transformative power of prayer. Here are some key attitudes to cultivate in our prayer practice:

1. **Gratitude:** A sense of gratitude can help us appreciate the blessings in our lives and open our hearts to receive even more.

2. **Humility:** Recognizing our own limitations and imperfections can help us approach prayer with a sense of humility and openness.

3. **Trust:** Trusting in the divine can help us surrender our worries and fears and allow us to feel supported and guided on our journey.

4. **Love:** Cultivating a sense of love for ourselves and others can help us connect with the divine and see the world through a lens of compassion and kindness.

5. **Patience:** Recognizing that the fruits of our prayer practice may not come immediately can help us approach prayer with patience and perseverance.

Remember that cultivating a positive attitude in our prayer practice is an ongoing process, and that it requires a willingness to be patient, open, and curious. As we continue to cultivate these attitudes, we may find that prayer becomes an even more powerful tool for transformation and growth in our lives.

Praying with Sincerity and Authenticity

When we approach prayer with sincerity and authenticity, we open ourselves up to a deeper connection with the divine. Here are some ways to cultivate sincerity and authenticity in our prayer practice:

1. **Honesty:** Being honest with ourselves and with the divine can help us approach prayer with sincerity and authenticity.

2. **Vulnerability:** Allowing ourselves to be vulnerable in prayer can help us connect with the divine on a deeper level.

3. **Authenticity:** Being true to ourselves and our beliefs can help us approach prayer with a sense of authenticity and integrity.

4. **Presence:** Cultivating a sense of presence and awareness in our prayer practice can help us connect with the divine in a more meaningful way.

5. **Openness:** Approaching prayer with an open heart and mind can help us receive the guidance and wisdom that we seek.

Remember that prayer is not about putting on a show or impressing others, but about cultivating a sincere and authentic connection with the divine. As we continue to practice with sincerity and authenticity, we may find that prayer becomes an even more powerful tool for growth and transformation in our lives.

Learning to Listen

Prayer is not just about speaking to the divine, but also about listening for guidance and wisdom. Learning to listen can help us deepen our connection with the divine and gain a greater sense of clarity and purpose. Here are some ways to cultivate the ability to listen in our prayer practice.

1. **Stillness:** Cultivating a sense of stillness and silence in our prayer practice can help us better hear the guidance and wisdom of the divine.

2. **Patience:** Being patient and open to the guidance and wisdom that may come can help us develop a greater sense of listening in our prayer practice.

3. **Curiosity:** Approaching prayer with a sense of curiosity and wonder can help us remain open to the guidance and wisdom of the divine.

4. **Intuition:** Learning to trust our intuition can help us better discern the guidance and wisdom that may come in our prayer practice.

5. **Practice:** Like any skill, the ability to listen takes practice. As we continue to practice, we may find that our ability to listen deepens and grows.

Remember that listening is not just about hearing words, but about tuning into the deeper wisdom and guidance of the divine. As we continue to cultivate the ability to listen, we may find that prayer becomes an even more powerful tool for transformation and growth in our lives.

Chapter 6
The Methods of Prayer

"The Methods of Prayer are many, but the essence of prayer remains the same - to connect with the divine and access the transformative power of the universe."

There are many different methods of prayer that we can use to connect with the divine and access the transformative power of the universe. In this chapter, we will explore some of the most common methods of prayer, including:

1. Intercessory prayer
2. Contemplative prayer
3. Meditative prayer
4. Praying with Scripture
5. Gratitude prayer
6. Affirmative prayer
7. Creative prayer

Each of these methods of prayer has its own unique benefits and can help us connect with the divine in different ways. By exploring and experimenting with different methods of prayer, we can find the ones that resonate most deeply with us and help us cultivate a deeper sense of connection with the divine.

Remember that the ultimate goal of prayer is not just to connect with the divine, but also to transform ourselves and the world around us. As we continue to explore the different methods of prayer, we may find that prayer becomes an even more powerful tool for growth and transformation in our lives.

Description of the Different Methods of Prayer

Here are brief descriptions of the different methods of prayer listed above:

1. **Intercessory prayer:** A form of prayer that asks for divine intervention on behalf of others, often used in times of crisis or need.

2. **Contemplative prayer:** A prayer method that involves quieting the mind and heart in order to connect with the divine and experience a sense of inner peace.

3. **Meditative prayer:** A prayer method that involves focusing the mind on a specific word, phrase, or image in order to deepen our sense of connection with the divine.

4. **Praying with Scripture:** A prayer method that involves reading and reflecting on sacred texts in order to deepen our understanding of the divine and our relationship with it.

5. **Gratitude prayer:** A prayer method that involves expressing thanks and appreciation for the blessings in our lives, as a way to cultivate a sense of joy and abundance.

6. **Affirmative prayer:** A prayer method that involves speaking words of faith and positivity, affirming the goodness and power of the divine within and around us.

7. **Creative prayer:** A prayer method that involves using creative expressions such as art, music, or movement as a way to connect with the divine and express our deepest emotions and desires.

Remember that each of these prayer methods can be customized and adapted to fit your individual needs and preferences. By experimenting with different prayer methods and finding the ones that resonate most deeply with you, you can develop a more meaningful and transformative prayer practice.

How to Choose a Prayer Method

Choosing a prayer method can be a deeply personal and individualized process. Here are some steps you can take to help you find the prayer method that works best for you:

1. **Reflect on your goals and intentions for prayer.** Do you want to cultivate a sense of inner peace and calm? Do you want to connect with the divine in a more meaningful way? Do you want to pray for a specific intention or request?

2. **Consider your personal preferences.** Are you someone who enjoys silence and stillness, or do you prefer more active and creative expressions of prayer? Do you feel more connected to the divine through Scripture or through nature?

3. **Explore different prayer methods.** Take time to research and experiment with different prayer methods, such as those listed in the previous answer. Attend different prayer services or workshops, or read books and articles on prayer methods to get a sense of what resonates most deeply with you.

4. **Listen to your intuition.** Ultimately, the prayer method that is most effective for you is the one that feels right in your heart and resonates with your spirit. Trust your intuition and don't be afraid to try new things, even if they may feel unfamiliar or uncomfortable at first.

Remember that prayer is a deeply personal and individual practice, and there is no right or wrong way to pray. By exploring different prayer methods and finding the ones that work best for you, you can deepen your connection with the divine and experience the transformative power of prayer in your life.

Combining Prayer Methods

While it's important to find a prayer method that resonates with you, it's also worth noting that you don't have to limit yourself to just one method. In fact, many people find that combining different prayer methods can be a powerful way to deepen their spiritual practice and enhance their connection with the divine.

Here are a few ways you can combine different prayer methods:

1. **Blend active and contemplative methods.** If you enjoy active methods of prayer, such as walking a labyrinth or using prayer beads, you can also incorporate more contemplative methods, such as centering prayer or mindfulness meditation, to help you deepen your inner awareness and connection with the divine.

2. **Combine different traditions.** If you come from a specific religious tradition, you can still explore other prayer methods from different traditions. For example, you might incorporate the use of mantras or chants from Eastern traditions into your daily prayer practice.

3. **Use different methods for different purposes.** You might find that different prayer methods work best for different purposes or intentions. For example, you might use lectio divine or Scripture meditation to deepen your understanding of a specific passage or prayer, and then use centering prayer or mindfulness meditation to quiet your mind and connect with the divine.

Remember, the most important thing is to find prayer methods that resonate with your heart and spirit. Don't be afraid to experiment and try new things, and trust your intuition to guide you in finding the prayer methods that work best for you.

PART III: DEEPENING YOUR PRAYER LIFE

"Deepening your prayer life requires not just more time, but a greater intentionality to connect with the divine. It's a journey of discovering the beauty and mystery of the divine, and allowing that connection to transform you from the inside out."

Chapter 7
The Power of Prayer

"The power of prayer lies not in the words we speak, but in the connection we make with the divine. It is a source of strength, comfort, and guidance that can transform our lives and bring light into even the darkest of moments."

Prayer has the ability to transform our lives in powerful ways. In this chapter, we'll explore the ways in which prayer can bring about change in our lives, as well as the world around us. We'll also look at some of the scientific research that has been conducted on the effects of prayer on health and well-being. Finally, we'll examine the ways in which prayer can be used to effect positive change in our communities and the world at large.

The Role of Faith in Prayer

Faith is an integral part of prayer, and it plays a significant role in shaping one's prayer life. Faith can be defined as complete trust or confidence in someone or something, and when it comes to prayer, faith refers to the belief in a higher power or divine force that is listening and responding to our prayers. Without faith, prayer can become a meaningless or even frustrating experience.

Faith allows individuals to approach prayer with a sense of hope and expectation that their prayers will be answered. When praying, one's faith can help to build a sense of peace and confidence, knowing that they are not alone in their struggles or concerns. Faith also helps individuals to be patient and persistent in their prayers, trusting that their requests will be answered in due time.

Ultimately, faith in prayer can deepen an individual's relationship with their higher power, allowing them to connect on a deeper level and experience a greater sense of purpose and meaning in their lives. Prayer can be a powerful tool for spiritual growth, and faith can help to enhance the experience and provide a sense of comfort and guidance through life's challenges.

Praying for Others

Prayer is not just about personal reflection and growth; it is also a powerful tool for helping others.

Prayer for others is a powerful act of love and compassion. When we pray for others, we are putting their needs before our own and asking for God's help, guidance, and protection for them. It is a selfless act that can help to lift others up, bring them comfort and healing, and show them that they are not alone.

There are many different ways to pray for others. Some people pray for specific needs, such as healing from illness, strength during a difficult time, or guidance in making an important decision. Others may simply pray for someone's overall well-being and happiness.

Whatever the reason for our prayers, the act of praying for others can have a profound impact on both the person praying and the person being prayed for. It can help to strengthen our faith, deepen our connection with God, and remind us of the power of love and compassion.

So, whether we are praying for a loved one, a friend, or even someone we don't know, let us remember the power of prayer for others and the role it can play in transforming lives and bringing hope and healing to those in need.

Praying for Yourself

Prayer for oneself is a deeply personal and introspective practice that involves communicating with a higher power or source of divine energy. This type of prayer can take many forms, from requesting blessings, guidance, or protection, to expressing gratitude or asking for forgiveness. In essence, it is an opportunity to connect with oneself and with the divine, and to seek comfort and support in times of need.

One of the benefits of prayer for oneself is that it can help individuals cultivate a greater sense of self-awareness and introspection. By taking the time to reflect on one's thoughts, feelings, and desires, and by expressing these in the form of prayer, individuals can gain clarity and perspective on their own lives and the world around them. This can lead to a greater sense of purpose and meaning, as well as a deeper connection with the divine.

Ultimately, prayer for oneself is a powerful tool for self-improvement, growth, and healing. By turning to the divine for guidance and support, individuals can find the strength and courage to overcome challenges, to cultivate positive habits and attitudes, and to live a more fulfilling and meaningful life. Whether practiced alone or in community, prayer for oneself can be a source of comfort, solace, and inspiration, and can help individuals navigate the ups and downs of life with grace and resilience.

Chapter 8
The Fruits of Prayer

"The fruits of prayer are not just the answers we receive, but the transformation that happens within us as we learn to trust, surrender, and align our hearts with the will of the Divine."

Understanding the Fruits of Prayer

Understanding the fruits of prayer involves recognizing the various ways in which prayer can impact our lives. Some of the fruits of prayer include:

1. **Spiritual growth:** Prayer can help us to connect with our spirituality and deepen our relationship with God. It can help us to feel more connected to our faith and to live a more meaningful, purpose-driven life.

2. **Emotional well-being:** Prayer can provide a sense of comfort, peace, and emotional healing. It can help us

to cope with difficult situations and find hope in times of distress.

3. **Physical health:** Prayer has been linked to improved physical health, including reduced blood pressure, lower levels of stress hormones, and a stronger immune system.

4. **Stronger relationships:** When we pray for others, it can help to strengthen our relationships with them. Prayer can also help us to forgive those who have wronged us, and to let go of anger and resentment.

5. **Greater sense of purpose:** Prayer can help us to gain clarity on our purpose in life and to feel a greater sense of direction and meaning.

Overall, the fruits of prayer can help us to live more fulfilling, joyful, and peaceful lives. They can provide us with the strength and resilience to overcome challenges, and the guidance to make meaningful choices that align with our values and beliefs.

How Prayer Transforms Your Life

Prayer can transform your life in many ways. Here are a few examples:

1. **It can bring a sense of peace and calm.** Prayer can help to reduce stress and anxiety, and bring a sense of calmness to your mind and body.

2. **It can help you to connect with others on a deeper level.** When we pray for others, we are sending positive energy and love their way, which can help to strengthen our relationships.

3. **It can bring a sense of purpose and direction.** Prayer can help us to connect with our inner selves and our higher power, and gain clarity on our purpose in life.

4. **It can improve our physical health.** Studies have shown that prayer can have positive effects on our physical health, including lowering blood pressure and reducing the risk of certain illnesses.

5. **It can bring us closer to God.** Through prayer, we can deepen our relationship with God and feel a sense of spiritual connectedness.

Overall, prayer can have a profound impact on our lives, helping us to live with more joy, purpose, and peace.

Integrating Prayer into Your Daily Life

Integrating prayer into your daily life is a powerful way to make it a consistent and meaningful part of your routine. Here are some practical tips for integrating prayer into your daily life:

1. **Set aside a regular time for prayer:** Find a time of day when you can consistently devote some time to prayer, such as in the morning, during lunch break, or before bed.

2. **Find a prayer spot:** Choose a specific place where you can go to pray each day, such as a quiet corner of

your home or a nearby park. Make this spot comfortable and peaceful, with minimal distractions.

3. **Use prayer prompts:** Create a list of prompts or reminders to help you remember to pray throughout the day. This could be as simple as setting an alarm on your phone or leaving notes around your home.

4. **Make prayer a part of your daily routine:** Find ways to incorporate prayer into your daily routine, such as saying a prayer before a meal, taking a few minutes to pray during your commute, or praying with a friend or family member.

5. **Use prayer resources:** Explore different prayer resources, such as prayer books, apps, or guided meditations, to help deepen your prayer practice and keep it fresh and engaging.

By integrating prayer into your daily life, you can make it a more consistent and meaningful practice, and experience the many benefits that come from a regular prayer practice.

Conclusion

In conclusion, prayer is a vital aspect of our lives, and it has the power to transform our relationship with God and others. Prioritizing Prayer: The Art of Making Prayer the Foundation of Your Life has been a journey of discovery, as we have explored the different types, methods, and benefits of prayer. We have also examined the obstacles that can hinder our prayer life and learned how to develop a habit of prayer. Moreover, we have looked at the heart of prayer, the role of faith, and the power of prayer, as well as how prayer can transform our lives and be integrated into our daily routines. Finally, we have explored the importance of the community of prayer and how praying with others can enrich our spiritual journey.

As we conclude this book, my hope is that it has helped you to understand the importance of prayer, to deepen your prayer life, and to experience the power and transformative nature of prayer. May you continue to prioritize prayer, and may it be the foundation of your life, as you journey towards a deeper relationship with God and others.